W9-AOV-274

The Material Culture of Steamboat Passengers

Archaeological Evidence from
the Missouri River

The Plenum Series in Underwater Archaeology

Series Editor:
J. Barto Arnold III
Institute of Nautical Archaeology
Texas A&M University
College Station, Texas

Maritime Archaeology: A Reader of Substantive and Theoretical
  Contributions
Edited by Lawrence E. Babits and Hans Van Tillburg

The Material Culture of Steamboat Passengers: Archaeological
  Evidence from the Missouri River
Annalies Corbin

The Persistence of Sail in the Age of Steam: Underwater
  Archaeological Evidence from the Dry Tortugas
Donna J. Souza

A Continuation Order Plan is available for this series. A continuation order will bring delivery of each
new volume immediately upon publication. Volumes are billed only upon actual shipment. For further
information please contact the publisher.

Library of Congress Cataloging-in-Publication Data

Corbin, Annalies
    The material culture of steamboat passengers: archaeological evidence from the
Missouri River/Annalies Corbin.
        p.   cm. — (The Plenum series in underwater archaeology)
    Includes bibliographical references (p.   ) and index.
    ISBN 0-306-46168-4
    1. Missouri River—Antiquities.   2. Excavations (Archaeology)—Missouri River.   3.
Underwater archaeology—Missouri River.   4. River steamers—Missouri
River—History—19th century.   5. Material culture—Missouri River—History—19th
century.   6. Material Culture—West (U.S.)—History—19th century.   7. Immigrants—West
(U.S.)—History—19th century.   8. West (U.S.)—Emigration and
immigration—History—19th century.   I. Title.   II. Series.

F598 .C67 1999
978'.01—dc21   99-048649

Cover photograph: The steamer *Helena* at the Milk River Landing in 1880 loaded with passengers.
F. Jay Hayes, photographer, # H-316, courtesy of the Montana Historical Society, Helena.

ISBN: 0-306-46168-4

©2000 Kluwer Academic / Plenum Publishers
233 Spring Street, New York, N.Y. 10013

http://www.wkap.nl/

10 9 8 7 6 5 4 3 2 1

A C.I.P. record for this book is available from the Library of Congress

The Material Culture of Steamboat Passengers

Archaeological Evidence from the Missouri River

Annalies Corbin

University of Idaho
Moscow, Idaho

Kluwer Academic/Plenum Publishers
New York • Boston • Dordrecht • London • Moscow